THIS BOO
BELONGS ...

Name: **Gracie R**   Age: **9**

Favourite player: **Messi, Ronaldo**

2022/2023

My Predictions...   **Actual...**

The Sky Blues' final position:

football	

The Sky Blues' top scorer:

4 / 2	6 / 4

Sky Bet Championship winners:

Sky Bet Championship top scorer:

FA Cup winners:

EFL Cup winners:

Contributors: Peter Rogers

A TWOCAN PUBLICATION

©2022. Published by twocan under licence from Coventry City Football Club.

ISBN: 978-1-914588-75-4

PICTURE CREDITS: Action Images, Alamy, Coventry City and Press Association.

£9

CONTENTS

GOAL OF THE SEASON

JORDAN SHIPLEY

Jordan Shipley's unforgettable strike against Queen Park Rangers was crowned the club's Goal of the Season, sponsored by Genesis Employment, for the 2021/22 campaign, after the academy product found the top corner in spectacular style.

The goal came straight from the training ground at The Sky Blue Lodge, with Shipley waiting on the edge of the penalty area to be picked out by corner-taker Todd Kane. The pass was perfect and met Shipley's boot asking to be struck towards goal. The shot was even better and was still climbing in altitude as it hit the back of the net, leaving David Marshall helpless to stop the effort.

The goal was Shipley's 20th and last in a Coventry City shirt with the midfielder swapping Sky Blues for the blue and yellow of Shrewsbury Town only months later. The goal beat off competition from Callum O'Hare, Gustavo Hamer and a number of his Sky Blues teammates to claim the prize.

RUNNERS-UP

Fabio Tavares came second in the Goal of the Season vote, for his last-gasp goal against Preston North End at the Coventry Building Society Arena.

The goal was his first for the club and secured the club a valuable point in stoppage time. The youngster has since earned a three-year contract with the club.

Matty Godden's opening goal against Derby County placed third in the end-of-season vote.

Godden and O'Hare demonstrated sublime understanding to work their way into the Rams penalty area before Godden picked out the far corner with an arrowed effort.

NUMBER OF SEASONS WITH THE SKY BLUES:

6

COVENTRY CITY LEAGUE APPEARANCES:

196

COVENTRY CITY LEAGUE GOALS:

39

PLAYER OF THE SEASON WINNER:

Never

LEGEND

PETER NDLOVU

SKY BLUES ACHIEVEMENTS:

11th-place finish in the Premier League 1993/94

MAJOR STRENGTH:

A wonderful dribbler who relished taking on defenders in one-on-one situations

INTERNATIONAL ACTION:

Peter was regularly capped by Zimbabwe during his Coventry City career

FINEST HOUR:

Scoring a thunderbolt winner against Aston Villa in the 1991/92 season

Top quality forwards Peter Ndlovu and Darren Huckerby were two of the most exciting wide-men to pull on the famous Sky Blue shirt and both made a big impression during their respective careers at Highfield Road.

Ndlovu and Huckerby were clear match winners on their day and were blessed with the skill, pace and talent to turn games in the Sky Blues' favour. With the ability to score goals and create chances for teammates, these two former Coventry City greats were both real crowd favourites at Highfield Road. Both players starred for Coventry in the Premier League era - but who was the best? That's for you to decide and here are a few facts and figures from their time in Sky Blue to help you reach your conclusion...

It's a tough call...!

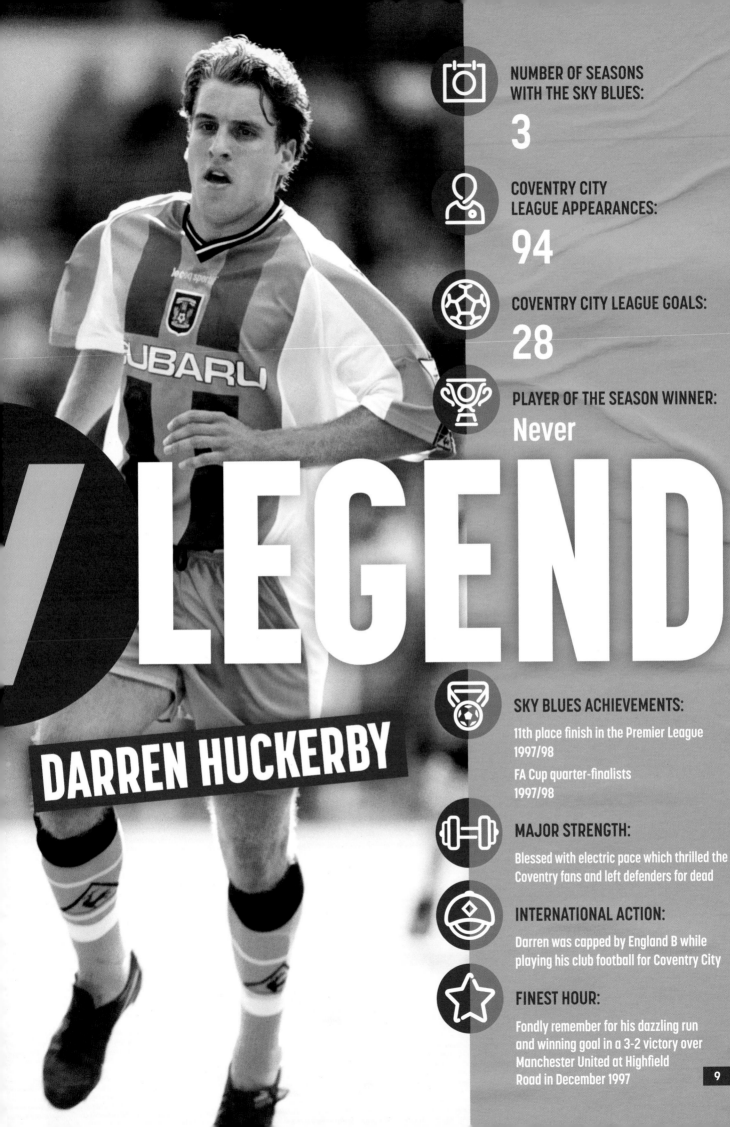

LEGEND

DARREN HUCKERBY

NUMBER OF SEASONS WITH THE SKY BLUES:
3

COVENTRY CITY LEAGUE APPEARANCES:
94

COVENTRY CITY LEAGUE GOALS:
28

PLAYER OF THE SEASON WINNER:
Never

SKY BLUES ACHIEVEMENTS:
11th place finish in the Premier League 1997/98
FA Cup quarter-finalists 1997/98

MAJOR STRENGTH:
Blessed with electric pace which thrilled the Coventry fans and left defenders for dead

INTERNATIONAL ACTION:
Darren was capped by England B while playing his club football for Coventry City

FINEST HOUR:
Fondly remember for his dazzling run and winning goal in a 3-2 victory over Manchester United at Highfield Road in December 1997

FANKATY

DABO

23

Defending is not just about stopping the attackers and clearing your lines. Making the best of possession you have just won is vital - although the danger has to be cleared, it is important for your team to keep hold of the ball.

SOCCER SKILLS
LONG PASSES

When passing your way out of defence, and short, side-foot passes are not possible, the longer pass, driven over the heads of midfield players, can be used.

EXERCISE

In an area 40m x 10m, A1 and A2 try to pass accurately to each other, with a defender B, in the middle between them. Player B must attempt to stop the pass if possible, and A1 and A2, must keep the ball within the area of the grids.

After each successful long pass, the end player will exchange a shorter pass with B before passing long again, thus keeping the exercise realistic and also keeping the defender in the middle involved. The player in the middle should be changed every few minutes, and a 'count' of successful passes made for each player.

KEY FACTORS

1 Approach at an angle.
2 Non kicking foot placed next to the ball.
3 Eye on the ball.
4 Strike underneath the ball & follow through.

Practice is the key to striking a consistently accurate long pass and to developing the timing and power required.

The same end result could be achieved by bending the pass around the defender instead of over him, and this pass could be practised in the same exercise, by striking the football on its outer edge (instead of underneath) which will impart the spin required to make the ball 'bend' around the defender - not an easy skill!

CHAMPIONSHIP
SQUAD

22/23

1 SIMON MOORE

GOALKEEPER   DOB: 19.05.1990   COUNTRY: ENGLAND

Moore joined the Sky Blues in 2021 following five seasons with Sheffield United, where he made 70 appearances. He arrived as a former Southampton academy product, who had past spells with Brentford, Cardiff City and Bristol City. His first season in Coventry (2021/22) saw him make 42 appearances as Mark Robins' top pick between the posts.

2 JONATHAN PANZO

DEFENDER **DOB:** 25.10.2000 **COUNTRY:** ENGLAND

Panzo will spend the 2022/23 season on loan with the Sky Blues from newly-promoted Premier League outfit Nottingham Forest. He joined having worked with assistant manager Adi Viveash during their time together at Chelsea, where Panzo started his career. Since then he has played for Monaco, Cercle Brugge and Dijon before returning to England in 2022.

3 CALLUM DOYLE

DEFENDER **DOB:** 03.10.2003 **COUNTRY:** ENGLAND

Doyle is making the step up to the Championship with the Sky Blues for the 2022/23 season, following a season spent on loan in League One with Sunderland last term. The Manchester City talent helped England to Under-19s European Championship glory prior to his arrival in Coventry and is tipped for big things in the future.

4 MICHAEL ROSE

DEFENDER DOB: COUNTRY: SCOTLAND

Born in Aberdeen, Rose made a name for himself in Scotland with his home town club before joining Coventry City in 2019. His first season saw him help the club to promotion to the Championship, making 40 appearances, and the commanding centre-back has remained central to Mark Robins' plans ever since.

5 KYLE McFADZEAN

DEFENDER DOB: 28.02.1987 COUNTRY: ENGLAND

Mark Robins' most experienced central defender, Kyle McFadzean has played at every level from National League North to Championship. He joined the Sky Blues in League One, from Burton Albion, and played a key part in pushing the team to promotion back to the second tier. He has made over 115 appearances for the club in little over three years.

6 LIAM KELLY

MIDFIELDER   DOB: 10.02.1990   COUNTRY: SCOTLAND

Liam Kelly's journey with the Sky Blues has taken him from the fourth division to the second, inheriting the Captain's armband along the way. The one-cap Scotland International has made 137 appearances for the club since joining back in 2017 and captained the club to promotion back to the Championship in 2020.

8 JAMIE ALLEN

MIDFIELDER   DOB: 29.01.1995   COUNTRY: ENGLAND

Signed by Mark Robins back in 2019, Jamie Allen had his best season in a Sky Blues shirt last campaign. After being made to fight for his place in the team, the 2021/21 season saw him make 41 appearances in all competitions. He is a tricky and dynamic midfielder who can create goals for his teammates.

9 MARTYN WAGHORN

FORWARD   DOB: 23.01.1990   COUNTRY: ENGLAND

After goalscoring spells with Rangers, Ipswich Town and Derby County, Waghorn joined the Sky Blues at the start of the 2021/22 campaign to help bolster Mark Robins' forward line. His first goal for the club came in a 2-0 win over Middlesbrough at the Coventry Building Society Arena.

10 CALLUM O'HARE

MIDFIELDER **DOB:** 01.05.1998 **COUNTRY:** ENGLAND

Callum O'Hare joined the Sky Blues from rivals Aston Villa following a successful loan spell during the 2019-20 season. Once his loan stay was made permanent, and with a League One winners medal around his neck, the creative midfielder kept hold of his place in the Championship and remains one of the club's most important players.

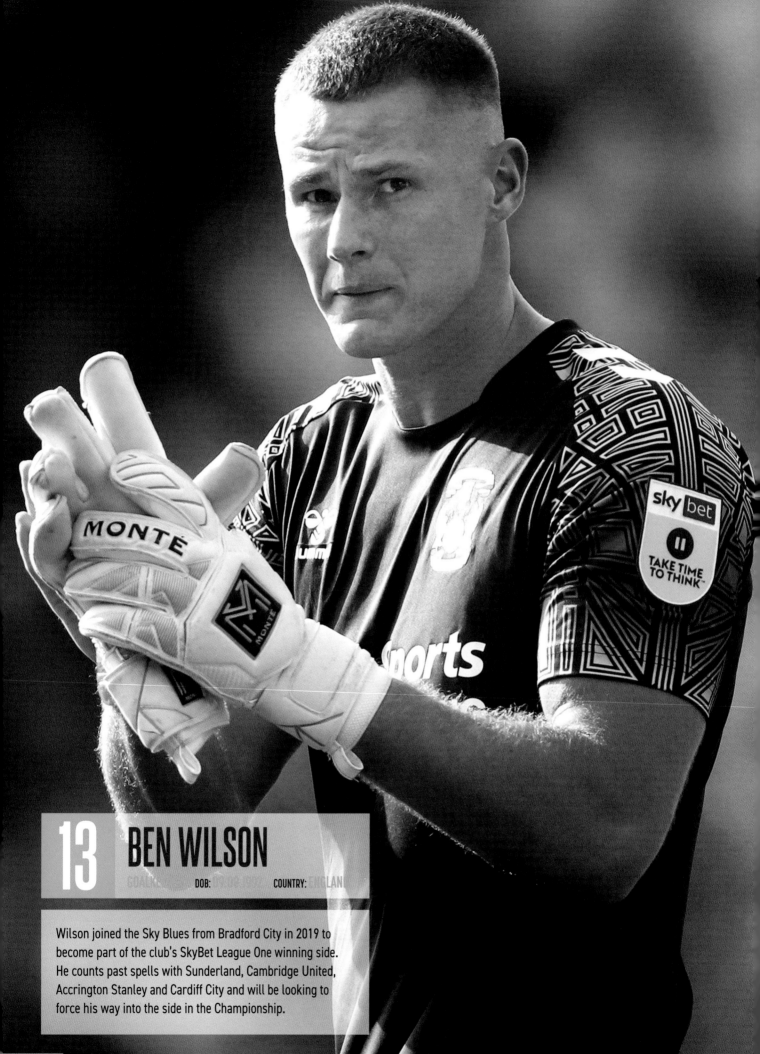

13 BEN WILSON

GOALKEEPER DOB: 09/08/1992 COUNTRY: ENGLAND

Wilson joined the Sky Blues from Bradford City in 2019 to become part of the club's SkyBet League One winning side. He counts past spells with Sunderland, Cambridge United, Accrington Stanley and Cardiff City and will be looking to force his way into the side in the Championship.

CHAMPIONSHIP
SQUAD
22/23

14 BEN SHEAF

MIDFIELDER **DOB:** 05.02.1998 **COUNTRY:** ENGLAND

The young midfielder joined the Sky Blues on loan, then newly-promoted to the Championship, in 2020 and saw his stay become permanent, signing a three-year contract, at the end of the campaign. The former England youth star has been a regular under Mark Robins ever since, scoring twice along the way.

COVENTRY CITY FOOTBALL CLUB

17 VIKTOR GYÖKERES

FORWARD   DOB: 04.06.1998   COUNTRY: SWEDEN

Swedish International, Gyökeres joined Coventry on loan for the remainder of the 2020/21 season, before making his switch permanent for the following campaign. His debut season saw him score just three goals in 19 games before he found form the following year, scoring 18 goals in all competitions and ending the campaign as the club's top scorer.

19 TYLER WALKER

FORWARD **DOB:** 17.10.1996 **COUNTRY:** ENGLAND

Walker swapped boyhood club Nottingham Forest for Coventry City back in 2020 after goal-scoring loan spells with Mansfield Town and Lincoln City. His debut season in Sky Blue brought eight goals and a further three following during the 2021/22 season before he joined Portsmouth on a short loan spell.

20 TODD KANE

DEFENDER **DOB:** 17.09.1993 **COUNTRY:** ENGLAND

The versatile Kane started his career with Chelsea, working under Adi Viveash, and arrived in Coventry ahead of the 2021/22 season. He scored his first Sky Blues goal in November, against Bournemouth, and went on to make 29 appearances during his debut season.

22 JOSH REID

DEFENDER **DOB:** 03.05.2002 **COUNTRY:** SCOTLAND

The Scottish defender joined the Sky Blues from Ross County in 2021 and will be looking to leave his mark on the first team over the course of the 2022/23 season. Reid, a left-back, spent the summer training with Mark Robins' group and featured for the club during pre-season. He has also been an important player for Under-21s boss John Dempster as they look to retain their Professional Development League title.

23 FANKATY DABO

DEFENDER **DOB:** 11.10.1995 **COUNTRY:** ENGLAND

Another former Chelsea star, Dabo has proved crucial for Mark Robins since his arrival back in 2019. The attacking right-back joined the club having turned out for previous loan clubs Vitesse and Sparta Rotterdam. He has since made 100 appearances for the club, helping them to win promotion from League One to the Championship.

24 MATTY GODDEN

FORWARD DOB: 29.07.19_ COUNTRY: ENGLAND

Godden enjoyed one of his best goalscoring campaigns during the 2021-22 season, scoring 12 goals in just 25 outings. His goals proved vital for Mark Robins and helped him to reach an impressive total of 33 in just 82 appearances for Coventry. He is Robins' natural finisher and loves an elaborate celebration.

27 JAKE BIDWELL

DEFENDER DOB: 21.03.1993 COUNTRY: ENGLAND

Former Everton defender Bidwell joined the Sky Blues from Swansea during January, signing a three-and-a-half-year contract that will keep him at the club until 2025. During his early months under Robins, he made 17 appearances and was a regular name one the team sheet during the pre-season of 2022.

28 | JOSH ECCLES
MIDFIELDER · **DOB:** 06.04.2000 · **COUNTRY:** ENGLAND

Coventry born and raised, Eccles arrived in the first team after graduating from the club's proud academy and played his part in helping the club to promotion in 2020. The following season saw him build experience on loan with Gillingham before returning to fight for his place in Robins' midfield.

30 | FABIO TAVARES
FORWARD · **DOB:** 22.01.2001 · **COUNTRY:** PORTUGAL

An exciting star of the future, Tavares scored his first Sky Blues goal in dramatic fashion when he found the top corner in stoppage time against Preston. Since then, the former Rochdale and Curzon Ashton striker has been handed a new contract with the club as he targets a leading role in Robins' strikeforce.

38 GUSTAVO HAMER

MIDFIELDER DOB: 24.06.1997 COUNTRY: NETHERLANDS

Coventry's midfield star, Hamer joined the club for a fee from Dutch side Zwolle following the club's promotion to the Championship. His talent was obvious from the moment he arrived and the Dutch-Brazilian playmaker has since scored eight goals in 85 outings. He remains one of Robins' most crucial players.

45 KASEY PALMER

MIDFIELDER DOB: 09.11.1996 COUNTRY: JAMAICA

Palmer started his professional career with Chelsea before impressive Championship loan spells earned him a permanent move to Bristol City. During the summer (2022), he arrived in Coventry with his sights set on helping the Sky Blues to promotion to the Premier League - and the 25-year-old has impressed during pre-season.

MULTIPLE CHOICE

Here are ten Multiple Choice questions to challenge your footy knowledge!

Good luck... ANSWERS ON PAGE 62

1. What was the name of Tottenham Hotspur's former ground?

A) White Rose Park
B) White Foot Way
C) White Hart Lane

2. Which club did Steven Gerrard leave to become Aston Villa manager?

A) Liverpool
B) Glasgow Rangers
C) LA Galaxy

3. Mohamed Salah and Son Heung-min were joint winners of the Premier League Golden Boot as the division's top scorers in 2021/22.

How many goals did they score?

A) 23 B) 24 C) 25

4. What is the nationality of Manchester United boss Erik ten Hag?

A) Swiss B) Dutch
C) Swedish

5. Where do Everton play their home games?

A) Goodison Road
B) Goodison Way
C) Goodison Park

6. From which club did Arsenal sign goalkeeper Aaron Ramsdale?

A) Sheffield United
B) Stoke City
C) AFC Bournemouth

7. What is Raheem Sterling's middle name?

A) Shaun
B) Shaquille
C) Silver

8. Who won the 2021/22 League One Play-Off final?

A) Wigan Athletic
B) Sunderland
C) Rotherham United

9. How many times have the Sky Blues won the FA Cup?

A) Once
B) Twice
C) Three times

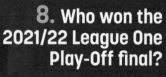
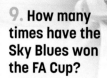

10. Which Premier League club have Coventry City loaned Callum Doyle from for the 2022/23 season?

A) Crystal Palace
B) Newcastle United
C) Manchester City

VIKTOR
GYÖKERES
17

CLASSIC FAN'TASTIC

Sky Blue Sam is hiding in the crowd in five different places as Coventry City fans celebrate winning the EFL Trophy in 2017. Can you find all five?

COVENTRY CITY
FOOTBALL CLUB

ANSWERS ON PAGE 62

LIAM
KELLY
6

Close control in tight situations creates havoc in opposition defences - particularly when receiving the ball in the air - and nine times out of ten, when a striker receives the ball, he has his back to goal.

SOCCER SKILLS
RECEIVING THE BALL

Quite often the ball will arrive in the air, and good strikers have to be able to cope with that - controlling and turning in one movement, ready for the instant shot.

EXERCISE 1

In an area 20m x 10m, two players A and A2 test the man in the middle, B, by initially throwing the ball at him in the air, with the instruction to turn and play in to the end man - if possible using only two touches.

The middle player is changed regularly, and to make things more realistic, the end players progress to chipping the ball into the middle.

The middle player is asked to receive and turn using chest, thigh, or instep.

KEY FACTORS

1   Assess flight early - get in position.
2   Cushion the ball.
3   Be half turned as you receive.

EXERCISE 2

A progression of this exercise is the following, where the ball is chipped or driven in to the striker from varying positions. He has to receive with his back to goal, and using just two touches in total if possible, shoot past the keeper into the goal!

To make this even more difficult, a defender can be brought in eventually. For younger children, the 'servers' should throw the ball to ensure consistent quality.

TRAIN TO WIN

Making sure that you are fit, healthy and fully prepared is key to success in whatever challenge you are taking on. Those three factors are certainly vital for professional footballers and also for any young aspiring player who plays for his or her school or local football team. The importance of fitness, health and preparation are key factors behind the work that goes into preparing the Coventry City players to perform at their maximum on matchday.

The Sky Blues players will need to demonstrate peak levels of fitness if they want to feature in Mark Robins' team. Before anyone can think of pulling on a sky blue shirt and stepping out at the Coventry Building Society Arena, they will have had to perform well at the Training Ground to have shown the manager, his coaches and fitness staff that they are fully fit and ready for the physical challenges that await them on a matchday.

Regardless of whether training takes place at the training ground or at the stadium, the players' fitness remains an all-important factor. Of course time spent practicing training drills and playing small-sided games will help a player's fitness but there is lots of work undertaken just to ensure maximum levels of fitness are reached.

Away from the training pitches the players will spend a great deal of time in the gymnasium partaking in their own personal work-outs. Bikes, treadmills and weights will all form part of helping the players reach and maintain a top level of fitness.

Over the course of a week the players will take part in many warm-up and aerobic sessions and even complete yoga and pilates classes to help with core strength and general fitness. The strength and conditioning coaches at the club work tirelessly to do all they can to make sure that the players you see in action are at their physical peak come kick-off.

While the manager and his staff will select the team and agree the tactics, analysts will provide the players and staff with details on the opposition's strengths, weaknesses and their likely approach to the match.

Suffice to say the training ground is a busy place and no stone is left unturned in preparation for the big match!

PLAYER OF THE YEAR

GUSTAVO HAMER

The Dutch-Brazilian midfielder went from strength to strength during his second season as a Coventry City player.

Hamer joined the club from PEC Zwolle in 2020 and immediately showcased his talent in a Sky Blues shirt - but had to wait more than a year before he could play in front of the Sky Blue Army, who took to him by creating his own song. The song could be heard ringing around the Coventry Building Society Arena and at away games, bragging of his talent and his bargain price tag.

During the 2021/22 season, the 25-year-old made 41 appearances and scored three goals, including a wonder-strike away against Peterborough United. He also scored against Swansea City, with his third goal coming in the reverse fixture against the Posh.

Hamer ended the campaign with ten assists to his name, seven more than he managed during his maiden season under Mark Robins behind closed doors. He was a regular in the Sky Blues XI throughout the campaign and proved vital in helping the club finish 12th in the final standings, their best finish since the 2005/06 season.

He remains one of the club's most important players heading into the 2022/23 season and is guaranteed to be ever-present once more in Robins' improving midfield.

YOUNG PLAYER OF THE YEAR

IAN MAATSEN

Maatsen joined the Sky Blues from Chelsea off the back of a successful loan stay with Charlton Athletic. He joined fellow Blues loanee Jake Clarke-Salter at the Coventry Building Society Arena, and his intervention proved dramatic as he quickly became a key player for the club.

Maatsen scored important goals against Fulham, Reading and Bristol City and left Coventry the following summer for a move elsewhere having made a lasting impact.

DREAM TEAM

Pick your ultimate Coventry City dream team and design them a kit!

win
mum

win
connor

win
Dione

and will do me

Ava esswe

win
me

win
messi

win
Ronaldo

Loser
Luke

Lose
bella

loser
Louise

loser
laila

loser
scarlett

JONATHAN
PANZO
2

BIRMINGHAM CITY

PRZEMYSLAW PLACHETA

A Polish international and true speed merchant, Przemyslaw Placheta is on a season long loan at St Andrew's from Championship rivals Norwich City.

The 24-year-old forward tends to operate on the left side of the Blues' attack and marked his home debut for Birmingham City with a goal in their 2-1 victory over Huddersfield Town in August.

BLACKBURN ROVERS

LEWIS TRAVIS

All-action central midfielder Lewis Travis was at the heart of Blackburn Rovers' impressive 2021/22 Championship campaign featuring in all bar one of the club's league games last season.

With the ability to carry the ball forward and help his team turn defence into attack, 25-year-old Travis has won many admirers for his energetic displays in the Rovers engine room.

BRISTOL CITY

ANDREAS WEIMANN

Austrian international forward Andreas Weimann was the Robins' leading scorer last season with 22 goals in 45 Championship games.

An experienced and proven goalscorer at this level, Weimann, who had scored goals at second tier level for Watford, Derby County and Wolves before moving to Ashton Gate, netted in each of the first three league games of the new 2022/23 season.

BURNLEY

JAY RODRIGUEZ

Now in his second spell at Turf Moor, Burnley-born forward Jay Rodriguez is expected to have a big role to play for the Clarets in 2022/23 as the club looks to bounce back to the Premier League at the first attempt.

A former England international, Rodriguez played top-flight football for Southampton and WBA before rejoining the Clarets in 2019.

BLACKPOOL

THEO CORBEANU

Blackpool signed Canadian international forward Theo Corbeanu on a season-long loan from Wolves in July 2022.

Standing at 6ft 3ins, the 20-year-old brings a real presence to the Seasiders' attack and was on target in both of Blackpool's thrilling 3-3 draws against Burnley and Bristol City in August and following the sale of Josh Bowler he could well be the go-to man for goals at Bloomfield Road in 2022/23.

CARDIFF CITY

MAX WATTERS

Exciting striker Max Watters will be looking to cement his place in the Cardiff City attack in 2022/23. After joining the Bluebirds in January 2021 from Crawley, Watters was loaned to League One MK Dons in 2021/22.

However, Cardiff boss Steve Morison has handed Max the chance to make his mark with a series of starts as Cardiff's got the new season underway in impressive form.

COVENTRY CITY

CALLUM O'HARE

Attacking midfielder Callum O'Hare enjoyed a highly impressive 2021/22 season and has gained the reputation of being both City's star performer and one of the most creative midfielders operating in the Championship.

With fantastic close control and superb awareness of teammates, O'Hare is blessed with great balance when in possession and the eye for a decisive pass.

LUTON TOWN

ELIJAH ADEBAYO

Elijah Adebayo topped the Luton Town scoring charts last season with 16 Championship goals at the Hatters reached the end-of-season Play-Offs.

A strong target man, Adebayo is expected to form an impressive strike partnership at Kenilworth Road this season with Luton new boy Carlton Morris who joined in the summer from Barnsley.

HUDDERSFIELD TOWN

JORDAN RHODES

Striker Jordan Rhodes has netted over 200 career goals since emerging though the Ipswich Town youth system back in 2007.

Now in his second spell with Huddersfield Town, 32-year-old Rhodes scored 87 goals in 148 outings during his first spell at the club. He returned to the Terriers in 2021 and scored the winning goal in last season's Play-Off semi-final against Luton Town.

MIDDLESBROUGH

MATT CROOKS

An all-action attacking midfielder who can also operate as an out-and-out striker, Matt Crooks joined Middlesbrough in the summer of 2021.

Signed on the back of a number of impressive seasons with Rotherham United, Crooks hit double figures in his first season at the Riverside and is sure to play a big part for Chris Wilder's team this time around.

HULL CITY

OSCAR ESTUPINAN

The Tigers completed the signing of Columbian international striker Oscar Estupinan in July 2022.

His arrival created a level of excitement around the MKM Stadium and the Columbian soon showed his capabilities with both goals as Hull pulled off a surprise victory over Norwich City in August 2022. A strong and mobile front man, Estupinan's goals may well help fire the Tigers up the table this season.

MILLWALL

BARTOSZ BIALKOWSKI

Polish international keeper Bartosz Bialkowski has been ever present in the Lions' last two Championship campaigns.

The 6ft 4in stopper is widely regarded as one of the most reliable goalkeepers in the division. Blessed with excellent reflexes, Bialkowski is an intimidating opponent in one-on-one situations and his command of the penalty area certainly provides great confidence for those operating in front of him

NORWICH CITY

TEEMU PUKKI

A Championship title winner on each occasion that he has played at this level, City's Finish international striker will be searching a hat-trick of promotions from the second tier in 2022/23.

A real threat in and around the penalty area, Pukki netted 29 goals in the Canaries' 2018/19 title-winning campaign and 26 two season later as they went up as champions.

READING

THOMAS INCE

A much-travelled forward, Thomas Ince joined Reading on loan from Stoke City in January 2022 and played a key role him helping the Royals retain their Championship status last season.

Playing under the management of his father, Paul, Ince Jnr then joined Reading on a permanent basis in the summer of 2022. His attacking play and appetite to shoot from distance have won him great popularity with the Reading fans.

PRESTON NORTH END

EMIL RIIS JAKOBSEN

Former Denmark U21 international forward Emil Riis Jakobsen enjoyed a highly productive 2021/22 season with Preston North End.

A powerful 6ft 3in frontman, he was the side's standout performer with 20 goals in all competitions last season. The 24-year-old is blessed with great physical strength while also displaying calmness in front of goal.

ROTHERHAM UNITED

DAN BARLASER

Goalscoring midfielder Dan Barlaser weighed in with nine goals in Rotherham United's League One promotion-winning campaign.

He progressed through the Newcastle United Academy and after gaining valuable experience on loan with the Millers he joined on a permanent basis in October 2020. Seen as the man that makes United tick, a great deal will be expected of the 25-year-old former England youth international in 2022/23.

SHEFFIELD UNITED

OLIVER NORWOOD

Northern Ireland international midfielder Oliver Norwood is something of a Championship promotion-winning specialist.

The 31-year-old has previously won promotion from this division with Brighton, Fulham and as a Sheffield United player in 2018/19. He scored his first goal of the new season as the Blades defeated Blackburn Rovers 3-0 in the opening month of the season.

QUEENS PARK RANGERS

ILIAS CHAIR

The creative spark in the QPR team, Moroccan international Ilias Chair chipped in with nine Championship goals in 2021/22.

A true midfield playmaker, Chair has the ability to open up the tightest of defences and pick out teammates with his exquisite range of passing. The skilful Moroccan is sure to be the man that new Rangers boss Mike Beale looks to build his team around.

STOKE CITY

DWIGHT GAYLE

Much-travelled goal-getter Gayle joined Stoke City from Newcastle United in the summer of 2022.

A nimble front man with the ability to score all manner of goals, his arrival at Stoke was met with great delight. While on loan at WBA in 2018/19 he riffled home an impressive 23 Championship goals and the Potters with be hopeful of a good goal return from their new signing this season.

CHAMPIONSHIP DANGER MEN

24 STARS TO WATCH OUT FOR DURING 2022/23

WATFORD

KEINAN DAVIS

Following an impressive loan spell with Nottingham Forest last season, Aston Villa striker Keinan Davis will be keen to help the Hornets push for an instant return to the Premier League having agreed a season-long loan at Vicarage Road.

Standing at 6ft and 3ins, the 24-year-old striker has pace and power in abundance and is sure to thrill the Watford fans during his loan spell.

SUNDERLAND

ROSS STEWART

On target in SAFC's 2-0 League One Play-Off final victory over Wycombe Wanderers at Wembley, striker Stewart riffled home an impressive 26 goals in all competitions last season.

The Scotland international wasted little time in stepping up to the plate at Championship level as he netted two goals in his first three league games of the new 2022/23 season for the Black Cats.

WEST BROMWICH ALBION

KARLAN GRANT

Former Charlton Athletic and Huddersfield Town striker Karlan Grant scored 18 times in West Bromwich's Albion's 2021/22 Championship campaign.

The 25-year-old appears to be the go to man for goals again in 2022/23 for Steve Bruce's men and has already been on target in the Championship and EFL Cup this season.

SWANSEA CITY

MICHAEL OBAFEMI

A two-goal hero in Swansea City's 4-0 thrashing of South Wales rivals Cardiff City last season, pacy striker Michael Obafemi netted twelve Championship goals for the Swans last season.

Having formed a great understanding with fellow front man Joel Piroe in 2021/22, Swans' boss Russell Martin will have great hopes for Republic of Ireland international Obamfemi again in 2022/23.

WIGAN ATHLETIC

CALLUM LANG

A product of the Wigan Athletic academy, Liverpool-born forward Callum Lang has firmly established himself in the Latics' first team as an attacking player with the ability to create chances for team-mates while also score goals himself.

The 23-year-old was in exceptional form throughout 2021/22 when he made 42 League One appearances and scored 15 as the Latics marched to the title.

MATTY
GODDEN
24

TRUE OR FALSE?

Here are ten fun footy True or False teasers for you to tackle!

Good luck...

ANSWERS ON PAGE 62

1. England star Harry Kane has only ever played club football for Spurs

2. The FIFA World Cup in 2026 is due to be hosted in the USA, Mexico and Canada

3. Manchester City's former ground was called Maine Park

4. Liverpool's Jurgen Klopp has never managed the German national team

5. Gareth Southgate succeeded Roy Hodgson as England manager

6. Manchester United's Old Trafford has the largest capacity in the Premier League

7. Jordan Pickford began his career at Everton

8. Huddersfield Town's nickname is the Terriers

9. Gustavo Hamer joined Coventry City from Feyenoord

10. Viktor Gyokeres netted 17 Championship goals for the Sky Blues in 2021/2022

43

NUMBER OF SEASONS WITH THE SKY BLUES:

7

COVENTRY CITY LEAGUE APPEARANCES:

238

COVENTRY CITY LEAGUE GOALS:

46

PLAYER OF THE SEASON WINNER:

Never

LEGEND

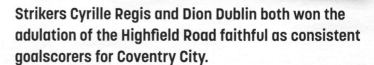

CYRILLE REGIS

SKY BLUES ACHIEVEMENTS:

FA Cup winners
1986/87

MAJOR STRENGTH:

A natural goalscorer who was
a threat to the opposition either
in the air or on the deck

INTERNATIONAL ACTION:

Cyrille won his fifth and final England
cap in 1987 as a Sky Blues' player

FINEST HOUR:

In November 1989, Regis became
the first Coventry City player
to score a winning goal at Anfield

Strikers Cyrille Regis and Dion Dublin both won the adulation of the Highfield Road faithful as consistent goalscorers for Coventry City.

Two powerful front men who led the Sky Blues' attack and embraced the responsibility of being Coventry's go-to men for goals throughout their Highfield Road careers. Both players possessed great physical presence and ensured that any central defender who was challenged with the task of marking them would certainly have known they'd been in a game.

Each player boasted an impressive goals-to-games ratio but who was the best? Well that's for you to decide and here are a selection of facts and figures from their time with the Sky Blues to help you make your choice. Once again, it's a tough call...!

LEGEND

DION DUBLIN

NUMBER OF SEASONS WITH THE SKY BLUES:
5

COVENTRY CITY LEAGUE APPEARANCES:
145

COVENTRY CITY LEAGUE GOALS:
61

PLAYER OF THE SEASON WINNER:
1996/97 & 1997/98

SKY BLUES ACHIEVEMENTS:
Joint Premier League Golden Boot winner with 18 goals 1997/98

MAJOR STRENGTH:
A great finisher with wonderful upper body strength that helped him lead the attacking line

INTERNATIONAL ACTION:
Dion Dublin made his full England debut as a Coventry City player

FINEST HOUR:
Scoring in the 2-1 win at White Hart Lane to help the Sky Blues survive on the final day of the 1996/97 season

CLUB SEARCH

EVERY TEAM OF THE CHAMPIONSHIP IS HIDDEN IN THE GRID, EXCEPT FOR ONE... CAN YOU WORK OUT WHICH ONE?

```
J B R A L G V N O R W I C H C I T Y M H
A I M O U Z E K F X R W F U C C D I S W
B R I S T O L C I T Y C B L A E S W P E
L M D A O H V E L P D N A L R E D N U S
A I D C N B E L W L O Q I C D W Y R L T
C N L I T U D R E I A V A I I Q P D O B
K G E T O U N U H P U W H T F I T E L R
B H S E W H E B N A I O L Y F M U T S O
U A B L N Y H T V R M J N L C H D I C M
R M R H U O T K L N C U S G I J J N Y W
N C O T M A R I Y O W T N D T M Q U T I
R I U A B U O T C A O I E I Y U R D I C
O T G N U F N S T A D P G M T M X L C H
V Y H A Y S N F C A E I K A S E M E E A
E I G G E G O I E K O S B C S Y D I K L
R A Q I L R T R P L U E N O A O E F O B
S H T W D Z S F O E G T X A D L R F T I
D B U R N L E Y R A S O A K W I B E S O
C O V E N T R Y C I T Y R F N S B H Z N
Q U E E N S P A R K R A N G E R S S A H
```

Birmingham City
Blackburn Rovers
Blackpool
Bristol City
Burnley
Cardiff City

Coventry City
Huddersfield Town
Hull City
Luton Town
Middlesbrough
Millwall

Norwich City
Preston North End
Queens Park Rangers
Reading
Rotherham United
Sheffield United

Stoke City
Sunderland
Swansea City
Watford
West Bromwich Albion
Wigan Athletic

ANSWERS ON PAGE 62

CALLUM
O'HARE
10

WHICH BALL?

Can you work out which is the actual match ball in these two action pics?

ANSWERS ON PAGE 62

NAME THE SEASON

Can you recall the campaign when these magic moments occurred?

Good luck...

ANSWERS ON PAGE 62

1. In which season did Chelsea last win the UEFA Champions League?

2. When were Manchester United last Premier League champions?

3. At the end of which season were England crowned World Cup winners?

4. In which season did Aleksandar Mitrovic net 43 Championship goals for Fulham?

5 In which season did Leicester City become Premier League champions?

6. When did Tottenham Hotspur last reach the League Cup final?

7. In which season were Sheffield United last promoted to the Premier League?

8. When did Manchester City win their first Premier League title?

9. During which season did Callum O'Hare make his Coventry debut?

10. In which season did the Sky Blues end their Championship campaign with a 6-1 victory over Millwall?

49

REWIND

SKY BLUES 2-1 FOREST

The Sky Blues returned to Coventry for the opening day of the 2021/22 Championship season, and they left it late to make it a memorable comeback against Forest.

After falling behind to a Lyle Taylor strike before the break, City pushed to get back into the game, eventually finding a breakthrough when Viktor Gyokeres scored his first goal of the season to level proceedings. Then, with the last kick of the game, Kyle McFadzean completed the turnaround when he fired the ball home in the 96th minute to send the Sky Blue Army into ecstasy.

FULHAM 1-3 SKY BLUES

Mark Robins took his side to Craven Cottage to take on the Champions elect, with Fulham looking to secure promotion back to the Premier League.

However, in front of a sell-out crowd, the home side would be left reeling when they fell two-goals behind in the first half, with Viktor Gyokeres and a Tim Ream own-goal putting City ahead. Bobby Reid pulled one back for Fulham, in what they believed would be a way back into the game, but ultimately it would be City who would go on to score again with Callum O'Hare netting in injury time to wrap up the points.

SKY BLUES 3-2 BRISTOL CITY

1-0 down and reduced to ten men just before half-time, the Sky Blues produced one of the performances of the season to beat Bristol City.

Ian Maatsen saw red, and Chris Martin scored the resulting penalty to put Bristol City in front, for a lead which would last until six minutes into the second half, when Matty Godden equalised from the spot himself. Weimann then put the Robins back in front for again only six minutes as Callum O'Hare scored his first goal of the season. Then, in the 92nd minute, the Coventry's ten-men of snatched all three points when Godden latched onto Liam Kelly's through ball to fire past Daniel Bentley.

FAST FORWARD

SKY BLUES V SUNDERLAND

25 FEBRUARY 2023

With only a handful of fixtures remaining in the 2022/23 season, the Sky Blues will welcome rivals Sunderland to the Coventry Building Society Arena for what promises to be a fierce Championship battle.

It remains to be seen where both clubs will find themselves at that stage of the season, but both the Sky Blues and the Black Cats will be desperate to claim the bragging rights of a rivalry that has grown since it's becoming in 1977.

SKY BLUES V BIRMINGHAM CITY

29 APRIL 2023

For the penultimate fixture of the 2022-23 season, the Sky Blues will take on Birmingham City at the Coventry Building Society Arena in a match-up that could define either side's season.

The two sides met late on during the 2021/22 campaign, with Coventry coming out 4-2 winners at St Andrews as Callum O'Hare performed his iconic sunglasses celebration. The Sky Blues will have to overcome a poor home record against Blues if they are to take victory, having failed to beat them on home soil since 2009.

BORO V SKY BLUES

6 MAY 2023

The day that will decide it all at the top and bottom of the Championship: Coventry City will face Middlesbrough on the final day of the 2022/23 season - and there could be an awful lot to play for.

Mark Robins' players will make the 180-mile trip north to the Riverside Stadium to lock horns with Boro, almost certainly backed by a bumper away following. The Sky Blues have not been to Middlesbrough and won since 1993, with goals from Peter Ndlovu and Mick Quinn, so must put aside that curse if they find themselves in desperate need of final day points.

1. Swii!

2. WHO AM I?

3. WHO AM I? Earlington

4. Marcus Rashford

ANSWERS ON PAGE 62

WHO ARE YER?

Can you figure out who each of these Sky Blues stars is?

5. Me!

6. Harry Cane

7. Messi

8. Ronaldo

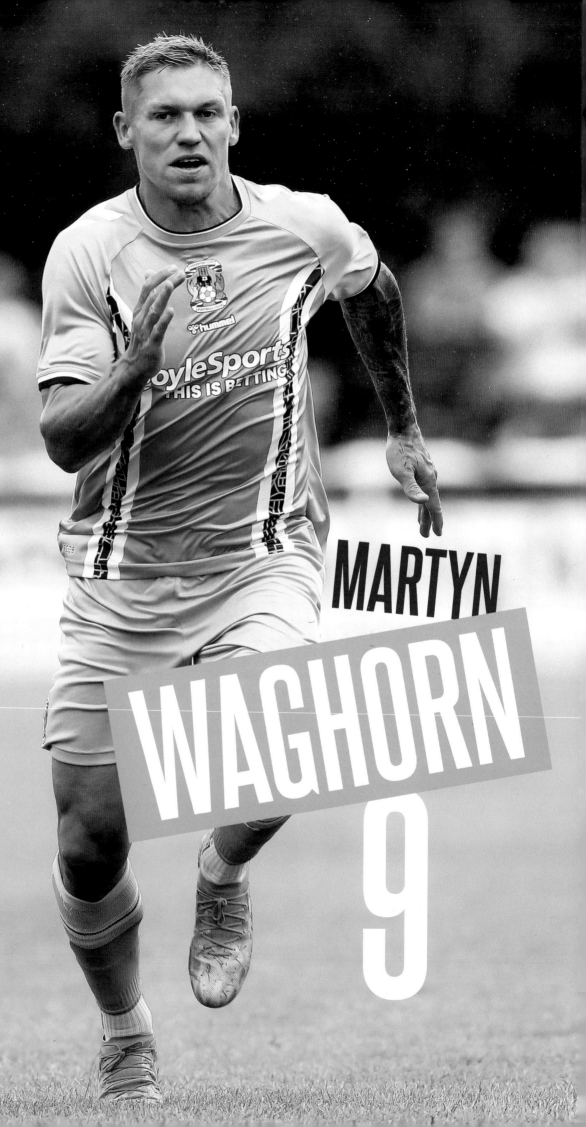

MARTYN
WAGHORN
9

girl virsion

COVENTRY CITY
FOOTBALL CLUB

TRUE
COLOURS

Can you colour
in this picture
of Martyn
Waghorn?

CHAMPIONSHIP WINNERS
Coventry City

PREMIER LEAGUE CHAMPIONS
Manchester City

FAST FORWARD>>

Do your predictions for 2022/23 match our own?...

CHAMPIONSHIP

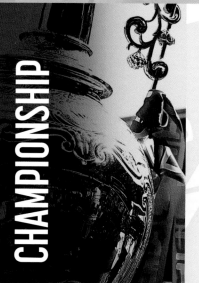

CHAMPIONSHIP RUNNERS-UP
Norwich City

PREMIER LEAGUE

PREMIER LEAGUE RUNNERS-UP
Chelsea

PREMIER LEAGUE TOP SCORER
Erling Haaland

CHAMPIONSHIP TOP SCORER
Matty Godden

LEAGUE ONE TOP SCORER
Conor Chaplin

FA CUP

FA CUP WINNERS
Spurs

LEAGUE CUP WINNERS
Leicester City

LEAGUE CUP

LEAGUE ONE CHAMPIONS
Derby County

CHAMPIONS LEAGUE

CHAMPIONS LEAGUE WINNERS
Real Madrid

LEAGUE ONE RUNNERS-UP
Oxford United

LEAGUE ONE

EUROPA LEAGUE WINNERS
Roma

EUROPA LEAGUE

NUMBER OF SEASONS WITH THE SKY BLUES:

16

COVENTRY CITY LEAGUE APPEARANCES:

507

COVENTRY CITY LEAGUE GOALS:

1

PLAYER OF THE SEASON WINNER:

1986/87

LEGEND

STEVE OGRIZOVIC

SKY BLUES ACHIEVEMENTS:

FA Cup winners
1986/87

MAJOR STRENGTH:

A big penalty-box presence who was
always happy to take command of his area

INTERNATIONAL ACTION:

Steve was widely regarded
as the best goalkeeper never
to receive an England cap

FINEST HOUR:

Despite never playing for England,
Steve was chosen in the Football
League's squad for a showpiece
match against the Rest of the
World at Wembley in 1988

Coventry City Football Club has a long
and proud history of fielding excellent goalkeepers
with club record appearance maker Steve Ogrizovic
and Swedish international Magnus Hedman both
starring between the posts for the Sky Blues.

As the last line of defence, both Ogrizovic and Hedman
produced a host of match-winning saves throughout their
Highfield Road careers while marshalling the defensive unit
in front of them. While Ogrizovic is the club's top appearance
maker, Hedman remains the Sky Blues' most capped
international. But who was the best? It's a tricky one to
decide and here are a number of facts and figures from their
time with Coventry City to help you reach your decision...

Yet again, it's certainly a tough call...!

LEGEND

MAGNUS HEDMAN

NUMBER OF SEASONS WITH THE SKY BLUES:

5

COVENTRY CITY LEAGUE APPEARANCES:

134

COVENTRY CITY LEAGUE GOALS:

0

PLAYER OF THE SEASON WINNER:

Never

SKY BLUES ACHIEVEMENTS:

11th place finish in the Premier League 1997/98

FA Cup quarter-finalists 1997/98

MAJOR STRENGTH:

An athletic 'keeper with great reflexes and superb anticipation of danger

INTERNATIONAL ACTION:

Magnus Hedman won 44 of his 58 caps for Sweden while plying his trade at Highfield Road

FINEST HOUR:

Hedman kept a clean sheet on his Sky Blues' debut in a memorable 4-0 victory over Tottenham Hotspur in December 1997

IDENTIFY THE STAR

ANSWERS ON PAGE 62

Can you put a name to the football stars in these ten teasers?

Good luck...

1. Manchester City's title-winning 'keeper Ederson shared the 2021/22 Golden Glove award for the number of clean sheets with which Premier League rival?

2. Which Portuguese superstar re-joined Manchester United in the 2021/22 season?

3. Can you name the Brazilian forward who joined Aston Villa in May 2022 following a loan spell at Villa Park?

4. Who became Arsenal manager in 2019?

5. Who scored the winning goal in the 2021/22 UEFA Champions League final?

6. After 550 games for West Ham United, which long-serving midfielder announced his retirement in 2022?

7. Who took the mantle of scoring Brentford's first Premier League goal?

10. Can you name the Sky Blues' defender who has been loaned to Shrewsbury Town for the 2022/23 campaign?

8. Who scored the final goal for Manchester City in their 2021/22 Premier League title-winning season?

9. Which striker joined Coventry City from Nottingham Forest in the summer of 2020?

JAMIE
ALLEN
8

ANSWERS

PAGE 26 · MULTIPLE CHOICE

1. C. 2. B. 3. A. 4. B. 5. C. 6. A. 7. B. 8. B. 9. A. 10. C.

PAGE 28 · FAN'TASTIC

PAGE 43 · TRUE OR FALSE?

1. False, Harry played on loan for Leyton Orient, Millwall, Norwich City & Leicester City. 2. True. 3. False, it was called Maine Road. 4. True. 5. False, Gareth succeeded Sam Allardyce. 6. True. 7. False, Jordan began his career at Sunderland. 8. True. 9. False, he was signed from PEC Zwolle. 10. True.

PAGE 46 · CLUB SEARCH

Huddersfield Town

PAGE 48 · WHICH BALL?

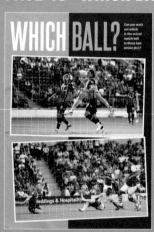

PAGE 49 · NAME THE SEASON

1. 2020/21. 2. 2012/13. 3. 1965/66. 4. 2021/22. 5. 2015/16. 6. 2020/21. 7. 2018/19. 8. 2011/12. 9. 2019/20. 10. 2020/21.

PAGE 52 · WHO ARE YER?

1. Jamie Allen. 2. Matty Godden. 3. Kyle McFadzean. 4. Viktor Gyokeres. 5. Fankaty Dabo. 6. Callum Doyle. 7. Jonathan Panzo. 8. Gustavo Hamer.

PAGE 60 · IDENTIFY THE STAR

1. Allison. 2. Cristiano Ronaldo. 3. Philippe Coutinho. 4. Mikel Arteta. 5. Vinicius Junior. 6. Mark Noble. 7. Sergi Canos. 8. Ilkay Gundogan. 9. Tyler Walker. 10. Julien Dacosta.